KNOW HOW KNOW WHY

CREATURES
OF THE DEEP

Written by Colin Dibben

Illustrations by John Francis and Q2A Solutions

TOP THAT

Licensed exclusively to Top That Publishing Ltd
Tide Mill Way, Woodbridge, Suffolk, IP12 1AP, UK
www.topthatpublishing.com
Copyright © 2014 Tide Mill Media
All rights reserved
0 2 4 6 8 9 7 5 3 1
Printed and bound in China

THE OCEAN AND THE WORLD

Earth was just another big rock flying through space 4.5 billion years ago. Then buzzing chemical clouds created water, lots of it. The world became a giant ocean – and life began.

How did the first ocean create life

The first ocean was full of tiny chemical particles. Two billion years ago, these particles formed living cells. The first life forms were bacteria and algae that 'ate' poisonous gases – like hydrogen sulphide and carbon dioxide – and 'pooed' oxygen. These bacteria and algae made the world inhabitable for other creatures.

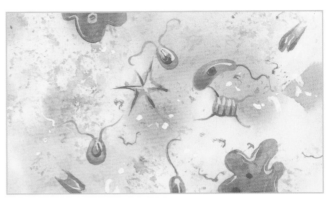

Earth's earliest life forms

What creatures lived in the primeval oceans

Had you been around 400 million years ago, you could have swum with armoured fish and crab-like creatures called trilobites. When dinosaurs ruled Earth, 230 million years ago, marine reptiles called plesiosaurs swam in the oceans. The 20 m (65 ft) shark, called megalodon, ate whales for breakfast 20 million years ago!

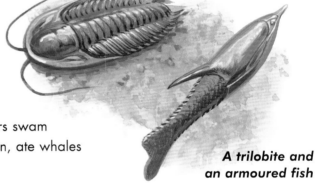

A trilobite and an armoured fish

The megalodon shark grew up to 20 m (65 ft) long – that's as long as 6 cars!

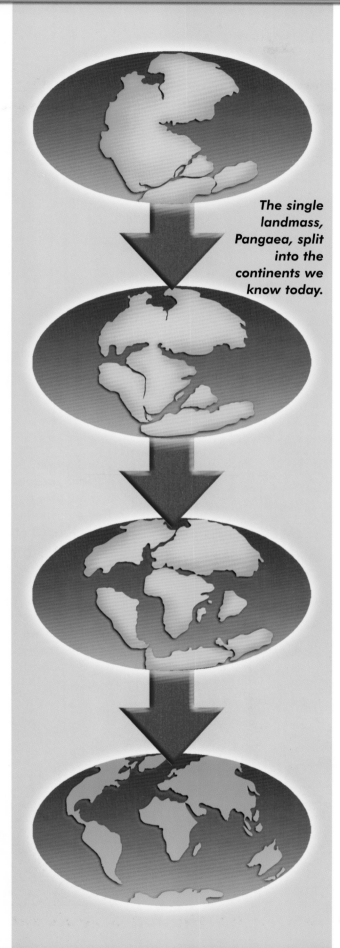

The single landmass, Pangaea, split into the continents we know today.

When were today's oceans formed

Until 250 million years ago, Earth's surface was a single landmass called Pangaea. Pangaea was surrounded on all sides by an enormous ocean called Panthalassa. Pangaea was torn apart by volcanic activity and eventually became today's five continents. As this happened, Panthalassa also split into five oceans.

Why are oceans important for life

Oceans are incredibly important for life on Earth because they provide most of the oxygen we breathe. Ocean currents keep the planet's temperature constant by absorbing the sun's warmth and moving it around the globe. Evaporation from the oceans helps to make rain – giving plants and animals water to drink. Scientists estimate that 230,000 forms of marine life are currently known, but there could be thousands more yet to be discovered.

FACT BYTES

Waves are caused by wind and tides. Tides are caused by the gravitational pull of the moon as it moves round Earth.

What are today's oceans called

There are five oceans: the Pacific, the Atlantic, the Indian, the Arctic and the Southern. Together they cover 70% of Earth's surface in salt water. Sea water is salty because of minerals, like calcium carbonate, dissolved in it. Calcium carbonate is found in animals and in rocks and sand.

THE OCEAN AND THE WORLD

LIVING IN THE OCEAN

The oceans are full of sea creatures of all different shapes and sizes. What's life like underwater and how do living things survive down there?

What do sea creatures eat ?

Marine animals depend on each other for food. This can be demonstrated with a food chain. It works like this: predators eat other fish; these fish eat tiny creatures called plankton; and plankton eat bacteria. The smallest plankton feed on sunlight and produce the oxygen that keeps all other sea creatures alive.

How do sea creatures breathe ?

Sea creatures need oxygen, just like us. Luckily for them, water has oxygen dissolved in it. Fish breathe through openings called 'gills' on their heads. Sea water flows into the gills and over blood vessels. Oxygen molecules move from the water into the blood – and are carried round the fish's body.

These creatures, in turn, become food for fish. Big fish eat smaller fish. At the top of the food chain are large predatory fish such as sharks, together with mammals such as sea lions as well as some species of seabirds.

Sea creatures need oxygen, just like us.

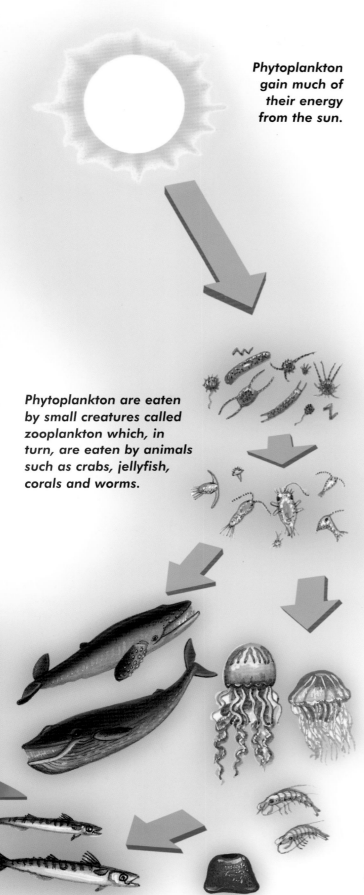

Phytoplankton gain much of their energy from the sun.

Phytoplankton are eaten by small creatures called zooplankton which, in turn, are eaten by animals such as crabs, jellyfish, corals and worms.

How do marine animals protect themselves ?

Over thousands of generations, sea creatures have developed clever ways to protect themselves – and attack their prey. As we shall see, many animals use camouflage to blend into their surroundings. Others do the opposite: their bright colours are warnings to predators. Some use poison to attack prey or defend themselves.

Camouflaged sea creatures

FACT BYTES

The oceans provide 99% of the space available for life on Earth!

Why are fish that funny shape ?

Fish have no legs or arms and have a curvy or streamlined shape. This makes it easier for them to move through water. As you know from swimming, water is heavy – it weighs down or exerts pressure on you. Marine animals have a large body surface to withstand this pressure.

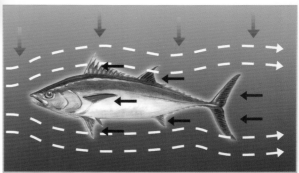

A fish's streamlined body

THE SUNLIGHT ZONE

**Dive into the sea and you are soon surrounded by soft, blue light.
The warm water is full of life. You are in the 'epipelagic' or sunlight zone of the ocean.**

Where is the sunlight zone ?

The sunlight zone stretches from the sea's surface to 200 m (656 ft) down – which is as far as sunlight can cut through water. Most sea creatures live here, including plankton. There is animal plankton and there is plant plankton. Plant plankton turns sunlight into oxygen by a process called photosynthesis.

FACT BYTES

All fish have a sense called the 'lateral line' that runs down their backs and picks up vibrations in water. This helps in detecting prey (and predators).

How do sea creatures stay afloat ?

If you live in sunny, warm waters, you certainly don't want to sink into the cold darkness below you. Sea creatures have large body surfaces that resist the water's natural tendency to push them downwards. Fish and whales also have oils or gases in their bodies to help with their buoyancy.

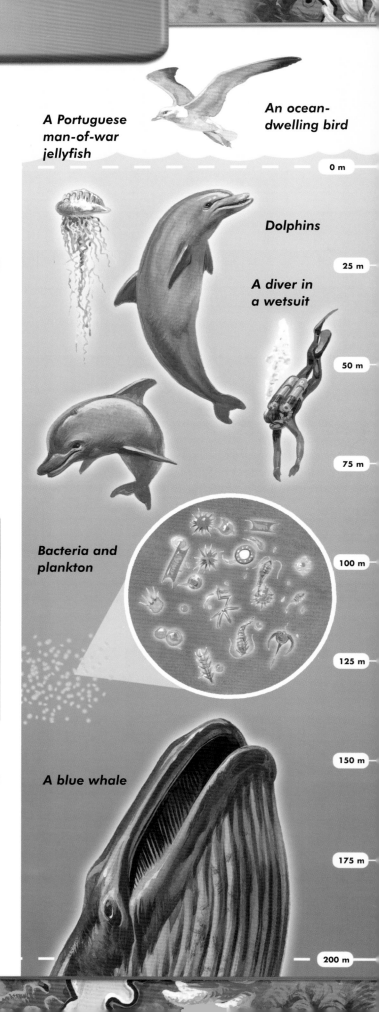

A Portuguese man-of-war jellyfish

An ocean-dwelling bird

0 m

Dolphins

25 m

A diver in a wetsuit

50 m

75 m

Bacteria and plankton

100 m

125 m

150 m

A blue whale

175 m

200 m

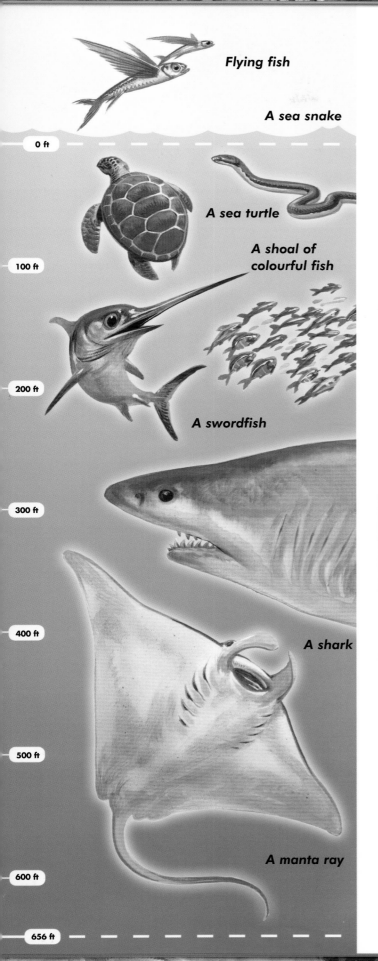

Flying fish

A sea snake

0 ft

A sea turtle

A shoal of
colourful fish

100 ft

200 ft

A swordfish

300 ft

A shark

400 ft

500 ft

600 ft

A manta ray

656 ft

Who lives here

Almost all the sea creatures you can think of live in the sunlight zone. There's fish of course like sharks, tuna and anchovies (one of the most common fish in the sea). There are also sea mammals like whales and sea lions, as well as squids, turtles and sea snakes.

What do they eat

Plankton is the most popular food source in the entire ocean. Predatory marine animals like sharks, sperm whales and seals eat small fish. The sunlight zone is the perfect example of an 'ecological system', in which different species live together and depend on each other for food, protection and survival.

FACT BYTES

Humans can't cope with sea water pressure. Our bodies collapse if we dive more than 70 m (229 ft) down – that's only a third of the way through the epipelagic zone!

Why does sunlight cause problems

The sunny sea is a great place to be – but there is one problem. Marine animals in sunlit waters can see what they want to eat, but this means that their predators can see them too! Sunlight zone dwellers are often a transparent bluish colour that helps them escape their enemies.

THE TWILIGHT ZONE

You'll need a special submarine to reach the 'mesopelagic' or twilight zone. Light doesn't reach this far down very much – and the animals start to look really weird!

What's life like in the twilight zone

Imagine if it was always 4.30 pm on a winter afternoon. The twilight zone is a bit like that! It's cold and dark and there's little food because there are no plants to make oxygen. The twilight zone stretches from 200 to 1,000 m (656 to 3,281 ft) – at which point light is completely extinguished.

Who lives in the twilight zone ?

Eels, octopuses, jellyfish and shrimp are common here. Other creatures like the lanternfish and the hatchet fish can be seen flashing on and off like traffic lights in the dark water. The firefly squid is a real show-off: it has three sets of lights on its almost 'transparent' (meaning 'see-through') body!

FACT BYTES

The cookie cutter shark has an extremely sharp set of teeth arranged in a circle. It can take a chunk out of a passing animal in a flash.

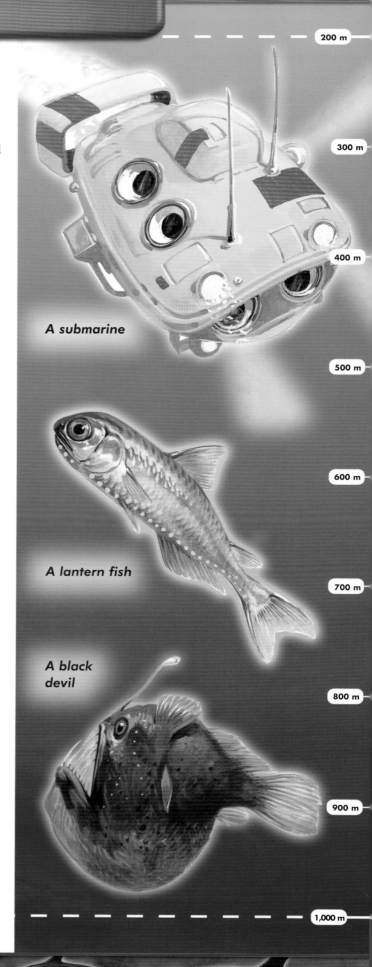

200 m

300 m

400 m

A submarine

500 m

600 m

A lantern fish

700 m

A black devil

800 m

900 m

1,000 m

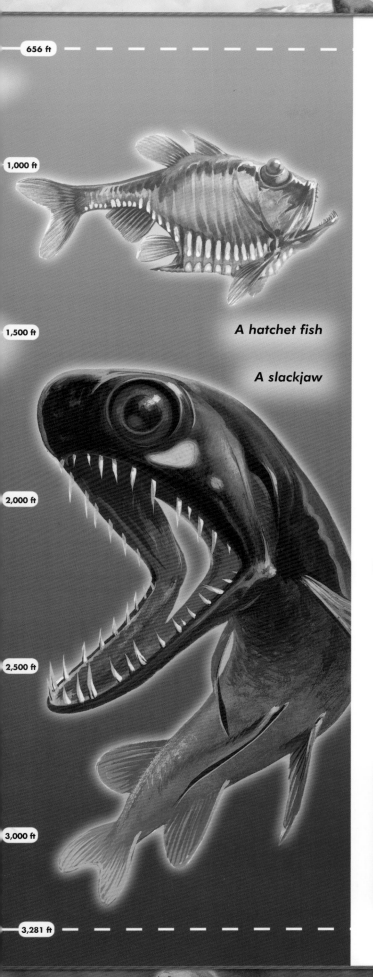

656 ft

1,000 ft

A hatchet fish

1,500 ft

A slackjaw

2,000 ft

2,500 ft

3,000 ft

3,281 ft

How do they see in the dark

Some twilight zone dwellers have really large eyes that can see up to 1,100 m (3,281 ft) down in the gloom. Many have special chemicals in their bodies that make 'bioluminescent' lights. These light the darkness, attract prey and provide camouflage from animals below them. Unlike electrical light, bioluminescence is cold.

What do they eat

Most sea creatures from this depth down eat something called 'marine snow'. This is bits of decaying food and dead animal that drift down from the epipelagic zone above. Predators like gulper eels and viperfish have long, sharp teeth and expandable jaws so that they can eat animals much bigger than them!

Why do fish go fishing ?

Here, food is so scarce that fish must conserve their energy. Predators don't waste energy chasing prey, they fish – hanging motionless in the water. Anglerfish use a glowing 'fishing pole' stalk on their foreheads as a lure, while viperfish use lights in their mouths to guide prey into their stomachs.

Squid rising to the ocean's surface at night

THE TWILIGHT ZONE

In the depths of the 'bathypelagic', night and day don't exist. The water is bone-chillingly cold and horrifying creatures haunt the blackness.

Where is the midnight zone

The midnight, or bathypelagic, zone is the biggest of the ocean zones. It stretches from 1,000 to 4,000 m (3,300 to 13,000 ft) below the ocean surface. The only food sources in the midnight zone are 'marine snow' and predatory killing. The only light is bioluminescent.

How do creatures cope with this harsh environment

Most midnight zone animals are extremely small. This reduces their need for food. They also have minimal skeletons, muscles and eyes – and don't swim very fast. They don't feel the water pressure because of gas or water in their bodies. They have thin skin, which absorbs oxygen easily.

FACT BYTES

The black dragonfish hunts its prey with a red light that most sea creatures cannot see – a bit like the nightscope on a rifle!

Why do animals need camouflage in the dark

You might not think that animals need camouflage down here where it's pitch black – but they do! At these depths, many animals are red because, unlike black, it does not reflect in bioluminescent light. Therefore, red midnight zone dwellers become invisible to predators.

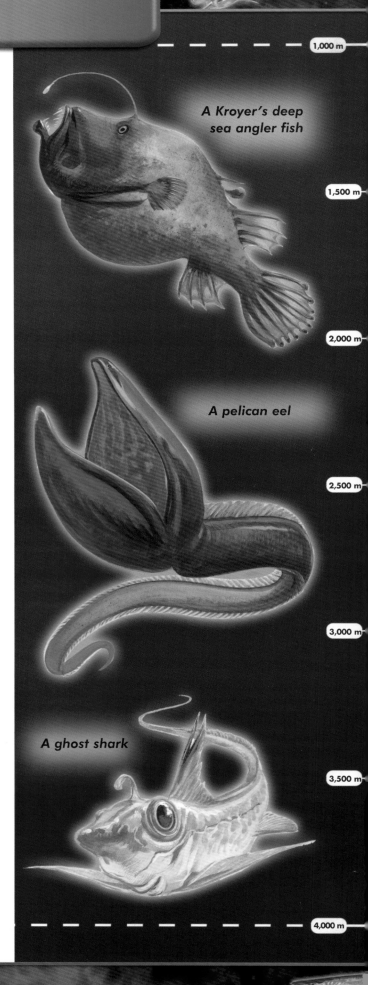

A Kroyer's deep sea angler fish

A pelican eel

A ghost shark

1,000 m

1,500 m

2,000 m

2,500 m

3,000 m

3,500 m

4,000 m

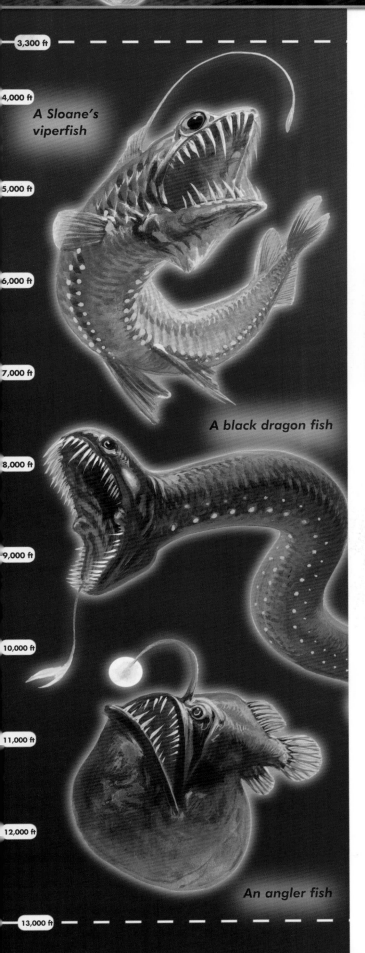

3,300 ft

4,000 ft

A Sloane's viperfish

5,000 ft

6,000 ft

7,000 ft

A black dragon fish

8,000 ft

9,000 ft

10,000 ft

11,000 ft

12,000 ft

An angler fish

13,000 ft

Who lives in the midnight zone

It's a regular horror show here! There are big critters like the sperm whale – which chases giant squid – but it's the creepy creatures that run the place. They have names like vampire squid, dragonfish, ogrefish, pelican eel, football fish and ghost shark.

A viperfish

FACT BYTES

The tube-eye or threadtail has a mouth that can expand to 38 times its original size as it sucks in sea water and food.

What are the creepiest creatures here

You are spoilt for choice, so dive in and take your pick! Vampire squid drop down on their prey, lacerating them with sharp-spined tentacles. Anglerfish have teeth in their throats to stop prey escaping. Pelican eels, or umbrella mouth gulpers, have huge mouths, which they open to swallow fish much larger than themselves.

A vampire squid

THE MIDNIGHT ZONE

11

THE SEA FLOOR

There's more life on the 'abyssopelagic' than in the two zones above it. If you want to live here, it helps if you like eating mud.

How deep down is the sea floor

The bottom of the sea is not a flat surface. The sea floor, which is also called the abyssopelagic zone, can be anywhere from 4,000 to 6,000 m (13,000 to 19,680 ft) down. The abyssopelagic zone is muddier than a football pitch in November, but is also surprisingly full of life.

FACT BYTES

Enormous sea spiders with 30 cm (11in.) legs can be found scuttling along the sea floor.

What is life on the sea floor like

The sea floor is made up of mud and ooze. Most of the creatures that live here are 'invertebrates', which means that they lack backbones. The brittle starfish sinks into the mud but keeps its tentacles out to catch food. Sea pigs get stuck in, eating the mud like earthworms.

Who swims over the sea floor

The transparent deep-water squid flounces through the water just above the muddy ooze, while the strange-looking flying sea cucumber uses its wings to zip about in all directions. The spindly tripod fish uses a set of extended fins as if they were legs – to avoid getting stuck in the mud.

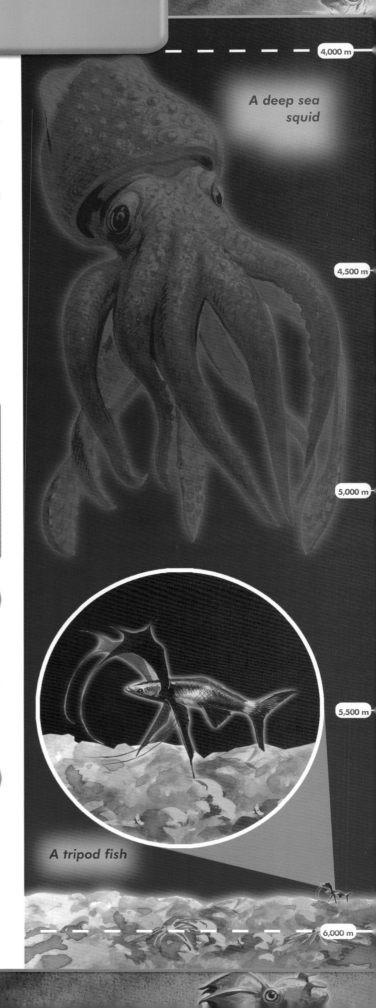

4,000 m

A deep sea squid

4,500 m

5,000 m

5,500 m

A tripod fish

6,000 m

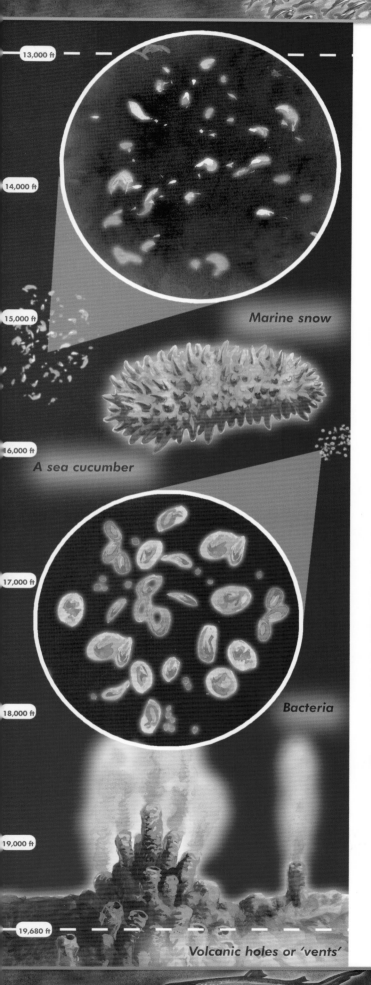

13,000 ft

14,000 ft

15,000 ft

Marine snow

16,000 ft

A sea cucumber

17,000 ft

18,000 ft

Bacteria

19,000 ft

19,680 ft

Volcanic holes or 'vents'

Why is life cool down here

There is more food and oxygen available on the sea floor than in the two zones above. The ocean's leftovers can fall no further and collect here. This marine snow becomes a valuable food source. The near-freezing temperature has a strange effect: it actually extracts more oxygen from the water.

FACT BYTES

If you put 50 football pitches end to end and stood them in the sea they would only just scrape the sea floor!

Where can you warm up on the sea floor

This ocean environment isn't always near-freezing. A food chain has developed around the hot volcanic holes or 'vents' that are scattered over the sea floor. Here, bacteria live off the poisonous volcanic gases. Small animals like snails and other molluscs eat the bacteria – and the snails are then eaten by crabs.

INTO THE ABYSS

There are immense rips in the ocean floor that lead even further down into darkness. Little is known about life in this most extreme habitat on Earth, the 'hadalpelagic'.

6,000 m	19,686 ft
	20,000 ft

The ocean floor
Height: 5,033 m/16,512 ft

Mont Blanc, France
Height: 4,807 m/15,771 ft

The Mariana Trench is deeper than the tallest mountains on Earth.

What is the deepest point in the ocean ?

The bottom of the Mariana Trench near Japan is 11,033 m (36,198 ft) from the ocean's surface. Trenches and canyons start to fall away from the ocean floor at 6,000 m (19,686 ft). The area between is the mysterious hadalpelagic zone – which is named after the ancient Greek word 'hades' – meaning 'hell'.

22,000 ft
7,000 m
24,000 ft
26,000 ft
8,000 m

How high is the water pressure ?

Water is heavy – and the more there is on top of you, the heavier it gets. At the bottom of the hadalpelagic zone the water pressure is immense. If you went down there, it would feel like you had 48 jumbo jets pressing down on every part of your body!

28,000 ft
9,000 m
30,000 ft
32,000 ft
10,000 m
34,000 ft

FACT BYTES

In 1960, two scientists in a pressurised submersible reached 11,000 m (36,000 ft) in the Mariana Trench – the deepest humans have gone in the oceans.

This really is the final frontier: scientists know much more about outer space than they do about deep-sea trenches.

Petronas Towers, Malaysia
Height: 452 m/1,483 ft

11,033 m	36,198 ft

Who lives here ❓

Life gets its foot in the door everywhere – even in the most inhospitable places. Starfish and tubeworms have been found at these depths. On the sea floor, tubeworms live near the volcanic vents, along with gigantic clams and mussels. Scientists think that the same animals live in the trenches.

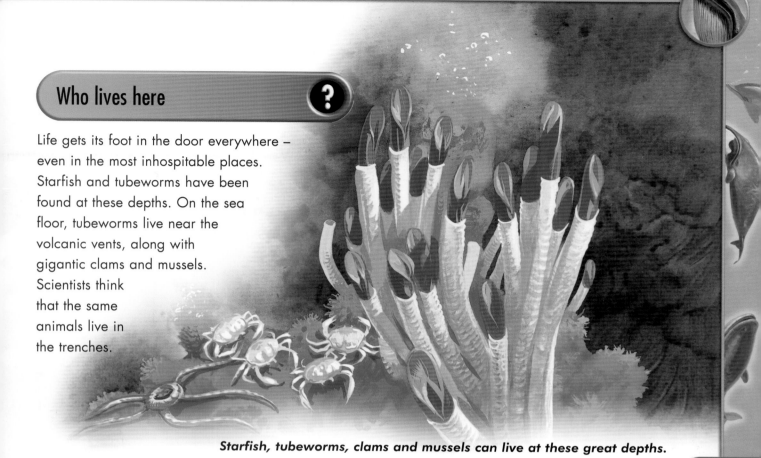

Starfish, tubeworms, clams and mussels can live at these great depths.

What's a tubeworm ❓

Tubeworms are very basic organisms – but can be bigger than a human. They are up to 3 m (8 ft) long and live in tubes attached to rocks. They have very simple bodies, without eyes, mouths, intestines or stomachs. They are hosts to the bacteria that turn volcanic gases into sea food. Scientists believe that tubeworms can live for hundreds of years.

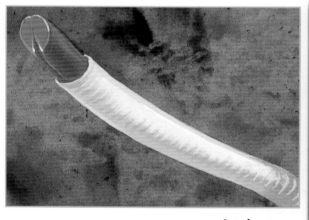

A tubeworm

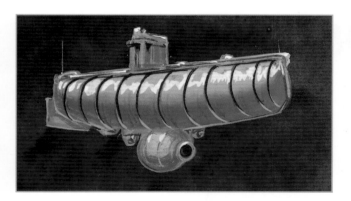

An unmanned submarine

Why are sea trenches so mysterious ❓

Sea trenches can be as big as canyons and are always incredibly deep. It is hard to get information about trenches because even the most modern unmanned submarines – called ROVs or 'remotely operated vehicles' – are difficult to manoeuvre in tight spaces. The extreme high pressure adds to the challenge.

LIVING IN PARADISE

In the warm, tropical waters off the coasts of Africa, India and Australia are some of the richest habitats in the seas: coral reefs that pulse and teem with colourful life.

Who lives in coral reefs ?

The coral reef is the greatest habitat – which means 'living space' – in the whole ocean. The reef is usually a small area, but hundreds of species live there. You will find angelfish nibbling on sponges, pufferfish bloating themselves with water, sharks, parrotfish, crabs, turtles and sea snakes.

Where can you live on a reef ?

Some Caribbean islands are coral reefs that have been pushed out of the sea by volcanic activity. Coral reefs also grow around extinct ocean volcanoes. The reef rises up as the volcano slowly sinks into the sea. The circular island or 'atoll' formed has a big hole in the middle.

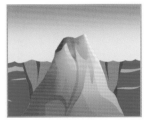
A volcanic island

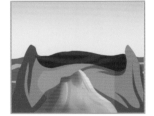
An atoll

FACT BYTES

The queen conch has a beautiful spiral shell that's lined in pink and up to 30 cm (1 ft) long. It is made from sea water minerals.

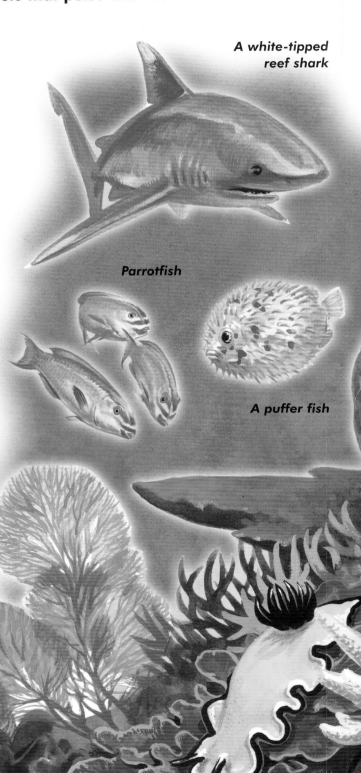

A white-tipped reef shark

Parrotfish

A puffer fish

Why are clownfish famous ?

Clownfish are the stars of the film *Finding Nemo*. Clownfish live amongst anemones, fish-eating animals that look like plants and have hundreds of poisonous tentacles. The anemone protects the clownfish from predators, while the clownfish cleans the anemone. This 'helping-each-other-out' is called 'symbiosis' – it's what coral reefs are all about.

What is coral ?

Coral reefs are huge masses of tiny tentacled animals called coral polyps. Young coral polyps settle on rocks and stay there for the rest of their lives. When a polyp dies, another grows on its chalky skeleton. Over thousands of years, the mass of skeletons turns into a reef.

A sea snake

Clownfish

Why are reefs dying ?

Coral reefs are dying because of pollution, disease, human activity and, most worryingly, rising sea temperatures due to global warming, and ocean acidification. Ocean acidification is caused by the increase in carbon dioxide in the atmosphere.

OCEAN OF ICE

The Arctic may look like a cold, white desert but under – and on top of – the ice there's a huge amount of sea life, from killer whales to furry seals.

Where can animals walk on the ocean

Usually an ocean surrounds a landmass, but in the case of the Arctic Ocean the ocean itself is actually the Arctic! The Arctic is a frozen ocean, which is totally covered with ice for most of the year. Mammals like seals, walruses and polar bears enter the sea to feed but live and give birth on the ice itself.

Why is there so much food here

During the summer months, some of the Arctic ice melts and there is constant daylight. This allows plankton to 'photosynthesise' all the time. This plankton explosion attracts billions of fish looking for food. The fish attract seals and whales from thousands of miles away.

Seals

A walrus

Orca dolphins

Who is the 'wolf of the sea'

The orca or killer whale – it's actually a dolphin! – is the most famous Arctic predator. It can jump onto ice to snatch seals, its favourite food. Orcas have earned their nickname because they hunt in packs like wolves. They reach speeds of 48 km/h (30 mph) and can live for 90 years.

FACT BYTES

Inuit hunters used the Greenland shark's teeth for knives.

There is no land under the Arctic. In 1958, a submarine travelled all the way to the North Pole under the ice.

What creatures inhabit this ocean of ice ❓

Harp and northern fur seals are some of the cutest inhabitants. Walruses with 1 m (3 ft) tusks sunbathe on the ice. The largest fish is the Greenland shark – it can be 6.5 m (21 ft) long and has bioluminescent eyes. The Greenland shark can break a hole through ice with its nose.

A walrus on land

Polar bears

A Greenland shark

Narwhal whales

What famous whales live in the Arctic ❓

The narwhal looks like a mix between a small submarine and a unicorn. Its tusk is 3 m (10 ft) long and is used for communicating with and fighting other narwhals. The smiling beluga whale makes so many funny chatters and clicks – even above the water – that it is called the 'sea canary'.

OCEAN OF ICE

THE BIG BITE

Sharks have been around since long before the dinosaurs. There are 368 species and they live in every ocean at almost every depth. They are famous for their teeth!

Why do sharks attack humans ❓

Few species of sharks attack humans – only the great white, tiger, bull and oceanic whitetip sharks do. They may mistake people for their favourite supper, seals. Sharks attack about 100 people each year.

What else do sharks eat ❓

Many sharks are carnivores that eat fish, squid, seals and sea lions. Flat sharks hide in the sand on the sea floor and pounce on crabs and clams. Other, larger, sharks swim with their huge mouths open to collect plankton.

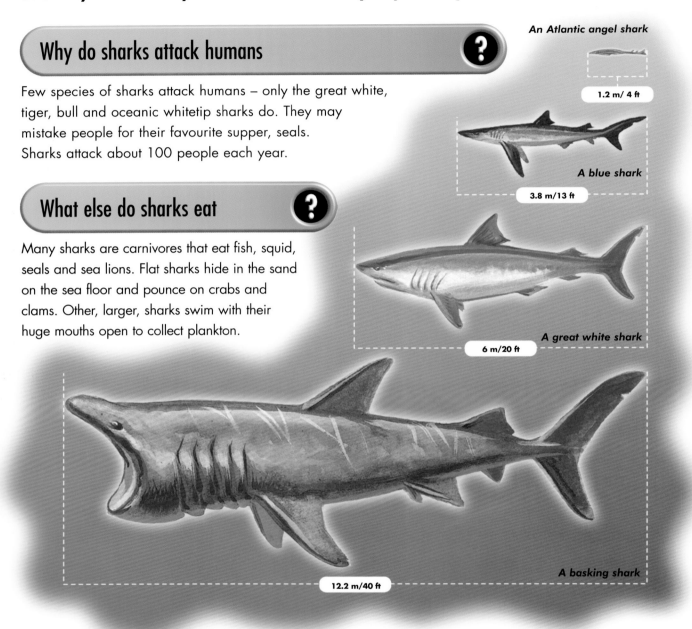

An Atlantic angel shark

1.2 m/ 4 ft

A blue shark

3.8 m/13 ft

A great white shark

6 m/20 ft

A basking shark

12.2 m/40 ft

A shark stalks its victim.

How do sharks hunt ❓

Sharks can sense lunch from more than a kilometre away. Unlike us, they hear and smell really well underwater. They are also able to see pretty well – and use their special fish sense, the lateral line system (and extra electrical sense organs called the ampullae) to home in on their unlucky victims.

Why are sharks called 'killing machines' ❓

Sharks are perfect predators. They are built to hunt and kill. Sharks have five rows of teeth – some rows rotate like a drill – and up to 3,000 teeth. These are triangular and sharp, with serrated edges – just right for taking big bites. When one tooth falls out, another takes its place.

A great white shark with a white-tipped reef shark

A shark's underside colouring (top) and upperside (bottom)

Why are many sharks blue ❓

Shark camouflage is called countershading and makes sneaking up on prey easy. The top of the shark is blue, making it difficult to see from above, because it blends into the water below it. The shark's white belly makes it difficult to see from below, against the lighter water above it.

THE BIG BITE

ROYALTY OF THE DEEP

Whales are one of the most intelligent and majestic creatures ever to live on Earth. They are also the only mammals that spend their whole lives in the open oceans.

What do whales eat

There are two types of whale. Whales with teeth, such as sperm whales and killer whales, eat fish and squid. Other species, like blue whales, grey whales and humpback whales have filters in their mouths called baleen. With these filters, baleen whales sieve the water for tiny shrimp called krill.

Where do whales live

Whales live in all the oceans, near the surface. They dive for food. Sperm whales can dive for an hour, all the way down to 3,048 m (10,000 ft). Whales often live in large groups called 'pods'. They make long migrations in search of food: grey whales travel 12,500 miles every year.

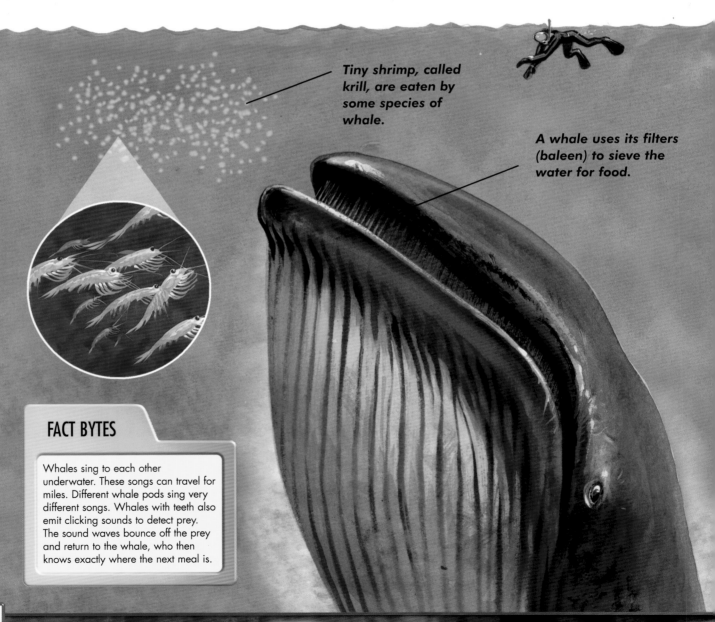

Tiny shrimp, called krill, are eaten by some species of whale.

A whale uses its filters (baleen) to sieve the water for food.

FACT BYTES

Whales sing to each other underwater. These songs can travel for miles. Different whale pods sing very different songs. Whales with teeth also emit clicking sounds to detect prey. The sound waves bounce off the prey and return to the whale, who then knows exactly where the next meal is.

FACT BYTES

Whales like to jump out of the water and bellyflop back down. They also like to stick their tails out of the sea and slap the water very hard. After diving, whales clear the blowholes which take air to their lungs – shooting a water spout 15 m (50 ft) into the air – the same as the height of 8 people end to end.

Why are many species endangered ?

For many centuries, humans have hunted whales for food and for the rich oil found in their bodies. This oil was used for burning in lamps. Other substances found inside some whales – like ambergris – were used to make perfume. Now many species are in danger of dying out and are protected by international law.

A whale shoots water out of its lungs through its blowhole.

FACT BYTES

Newborn blue whales weigh 2.25 tonnes!

ROYALTY OF THE DEEP

23

OUR BEST FRIENDS?

Dolphins are famous for being intelligent and friendly. You can swim with a school of 1,000 dolphins and they'll be as interested in you as you are in them!

How do dolphins talk ?

Dolphins like to whistle lots and stroke each other with their flippers. Dolphin mums teach each of their young a unique whistle. So when two dolphins meet, they are saying 'hi' and telling the other dolphin their name. Scientists think humans can talk to dolphins – by turning words into whistles.

FACT BYTES

Dolphins can often be seen 'surfing' the waves produced by boats. Dusky dolphins are so good at this that they can reach speeds of 56 km/h (35 mph), jump 6 m (20 ft) in the air and turn somersaults while surfing. This may help them catch fish – but it's also fun!

Dolphins are able to communicate with each other by whistling.

FACT BYTES

Just like whales, dolphins make noises called 'clicks'. They are produced by the dolphin's forehead and are actually two sound beams. These beams rebound off underwater objects and are transmitted to the dolphin's brain – where they create a detailed picture of the object. Dolphins also use 'clicks' to stun prey.

What is the major cause of dolphin deaths

In recent years, almost five million dolphins have been trapped and drowned in the enormous 'drift nets' that are set to catch tuna. Next time you're shopping with mum, check that the tinned tuna is 'dolphin friendly'. This means that the tuna was caught in nets that allow dolphins to escape.

Huge fishing nets can accidently trap dolphins.

Why are dolphins such good swimmers

Like all whales, dolphins move their tails up and down. Fish, on the other hand, move their tails from left to right. This may not sound like a big difference, but it allows dolphins to create a changing body shape in the water and slip through the water very fast.

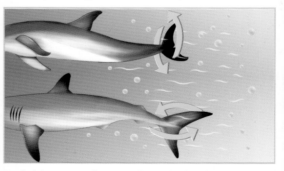

Dolphins use their tails to help them swim.

OUR BEST FRIENDS?

OCEAN GLIDERS

Rays are amazingly graceful flat fish that glide over reefs and the sea floor. They are related to sharks and are found in all oceans, often in very large groups.

Why do rays look so strange ?

Rays look as though they've been squashed! They have fins that have melted into their flat bodies to form discs. Rays also have long tails. The ray's skeleton is made from cartilage. The skeleton and the disc are great for gliding through water – and for hiding on the sea bed waiting for prey.

Rays have flat bodies.

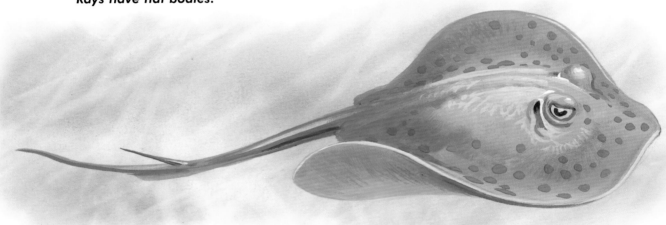

How do rays swim ?

Rays swim very differently from other fish. The tips of their powerful, wing-like fins ripple and flap, allowing them to glide gracefully through water. Some rays, like the mangrove whipray and the manta, can even jump out of the water. There are stories of manta rays squashing fishermen when they fly!

Rays can even jump out of the water.

Why do stingrays attack humans

Because stingrays are flat and often hidden on the sea floor, people sometimes step on them. The stingray then lashes its whip-like tail, which has serrated, venomous spines. Humans can have heart attacks after being stung. Always 'shuffle' through shallow, tropical waters to avoid being stung by a buried stingray.

Stingrays can hide on the sea floor.

How do electric rays hunt ?

It's not the tail of the electric ray that you have to watch out for. It is the muscles in its head that produce a large electric current – of up to 220 volts! The ray drifts over fish and then zaps them. The ray wraps itself around the fish to concentrate the electric field.

An electric ray

FACT BYTES

The earliest ray was called a guitarfish and lived 150 million years ago.

When a ray stops swimming, it sinks down to the sea bed.

How big do rays get ?

The manta ray is the largest ray. It looks like a spaceship and can be 9 m (29.5 ft) wide and weigh many tons. Mantas eat plankton, funnelling food into their mouth while they swim. They use the two flaps near their eyes like bendy chopsticks, to push food towards their mouths.

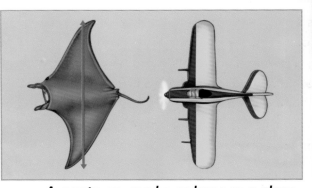

A manta ray can be as large as a plane.

SPINELESS GENIUS

They writhe and wriggle through the ocean, but squid and octopuses are really smart when it comes to staying out of trouble.

What are squid ❓

Squid and octopuses are sometimes described as 'humans without bones'. They seem to be all tentacles and a big head. They don't have skeletons, which is why they move through the water in such a funny way. They do have highly advanced nervous systems. Squid have ten tentacles; octopuses have eight.

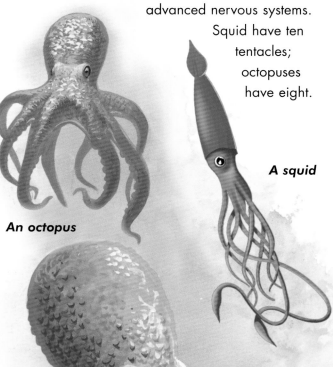

An octopus

A squid

An octopus with its prey

How do octopuses swim ❓

Octopuses and squid are pretty unusual because they both use jet propulsion to swim. They suck in water through an opening in the back of their heads, then force it out through siphons on the sides of their heads. They can speed along at up to 37 km/h (23 mph).

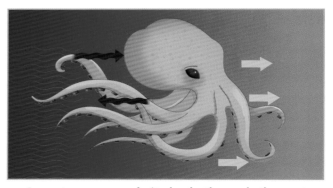

An octopus propels its body through the water.

What do octopuses eat ❓

Octopuses and their relations love to eat fish, crabs and shellfish. They grab food with their tentacles, which shoot out like harpoons and have lots of suckers on them to help the octopus grip. The prey is pushed towards the beak, which injects venom, breaks shells and cuts food up.

An octopus beak

How do they avoid predators ?

So many animals eat squid and their cousins that they need to have very good defences. Many octopuses can change colour to camouflage themselves or to frighten predators. Squid and octopuses are also famous for being able to squirt black ink at enemies. Some deep-sea species are transparent, which makes them almost invisible.

A squid squirts black ink from its body.

FACT BYTES

Octopuses live in caves and are very house proud: they use their siphons to squirt debris out of their homes after they have eaten.

FACT BYTES

Some squid can jump 12 m (40 ft) out of the water to escape predators.

Each octopus tentacle has 240 suction cups on it for grip.

A giant squid uses its suction cups to fight with a whale.

Where do giant squid live ?

Giant squid live between 200 m (700 ft) and 4,000 m (13,300 ft) down. They are not as monstrous as they look in films – but they can be 18 m (60 ft) long. Giant squid have been known to fight with sperm whales nearer the surface; many sperm whales have sucker scars on their skins.

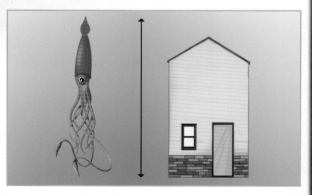

A giant squid can be as long as a house is high.

SPINELESS GENIUS

COLD-BLOODED KILLERS

Speed, power, adaptability, sharp senses and sharper teeth – these are what make a perfect predator. In the sea, where most creatures are cold-blooded, size really doesn't count.

Who is the best-adapted predator ❓

The most successful animals have adapted really well to their environments. The nudibranch takes this a step further – it actually adapts what it eats. This small, slow-moving sea snail eats jellyfish and sea anemones. The nudibranch incorporates their venoms and stings into its own body defences to use against predators!

A nudibranch

A jellyfish   *A sea anemone*

Who is the fastest predator ❓

The 20 cm (8 in.) mantis shrimp is the fastest predator on Earth. It spears or smashes prey with a concealed, reinforced forearm. The strike is as fast (8 milliseconds!) and as powerful as a bullet. The mantis shrimp is a real pest in aquariums – it is always breaking the toughened glass.

Which shark is the most dangerous ❓

Great white sharks have a bad reputation, but they hardly ever attack people because they live in the deep ocean. The bull shark, however, swims near beaches. It is very bad tempered and will attack anything. The bull shark can even swim up rivers and jump over rapids into lakes.

A bull shark

A mantis shrimp

Why do sharp senses help ?

The more precisely a predator tracks prey, the quicker it can kill and eat. Using its spade-shaped head, the hammerhead shark can detect a drop of blood in 100 litres (22 gallons) of water. The hammerhead swims towards dinner shaking its head. This tells it exactly where the target is.

A hammerhead shark

FACT BYTES

The viperfish (below) impales prey on its oversize fangs after slamming into it at high speeds.

How does the fiercest predator attack ?

The great barracuda lives on coral reefs. It is stealthy and lightning quick, with dagger-like fangs that tear, slash and slice. The barracuda's long body is flexible, allowing it to charge fast at its prey through twisting reefs. The barracuda has attacked swimmers – it is attracted to shiny swimming costumes!

FACT BYTES

The 2.4 m (8 ft) wolf-eel (below) has extremely strong jaws – perfect for crushing crabs.

A great barracuda

COLD-BLOODED KILLERS

THE BIG ONES

Being one of the biggest creatures in the sea isn't easy. You may not have many predators, but feeding yourself becomes a full-time job.

What is the biggest sea animal

The 30.5 m (100 ft) blue whale is the largest animal on land or sea – ever. It weighs in at a massive 130 tonnes, has a heart the size of a small car and eats 4 tonnes of krill every day. The underwater song of the blue whale is louder than a jet plane!

Which big animals have predators

Man is the only predator of most big sea creatures. One example is the sperm whale, which eats giant squid. The whale's stomach produces a sweet-smelling, precious substance called ambergris to counter the venom found in the squid's hard beak. Humans hunted the whale for centuries to collect this substance.

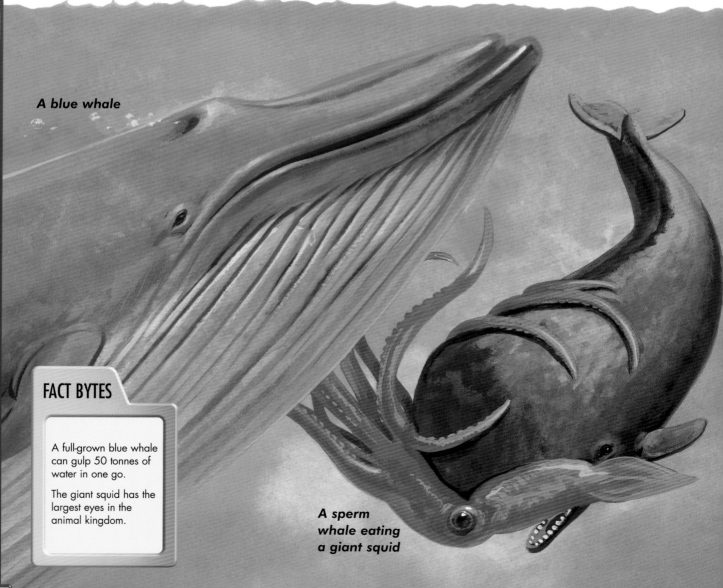

A blue whale

FACT BYTES

A full-grown blue whale can gulp 50 tonnes of water in one go.

The giant squid has the largest eyes in the animal kingdom.

A sperm whale eating a giant squid

Why do they migrate ?

Many species travel in search of food and breeding grounds. The 2.5 m (8 ft) great sea turtle swims thousands of miles to lay eggs on the same beach it was born on. Despite the weight of two skeletons (the shell counts as a second skeleton), the sea turtle is a great swimmer.

How do they stay afloat ?

Most big sea animals have enormous oily organs that keep them afloat. Walruses – which are up to 4.3 m (14 ft) long and can weigh 900 kg (2,000 lbs) – also have air bags in their throats. This helps them keep their heads above the water as they prowl the Arctic ocean.

A walrus

A sea turtle

A basking shark

How do big animals feed ?

The bigger the animal, the more difficult it is to chase prey. Big animals tend to vacuum up plankton – and are called filter feeders – rather than attack fish. This makes feeding easier and gives them time to relax: the 10 m (33 ft) basking shark likes to 'catch the rays' near the surface.

THE BIG ONES

BRINGING UP BABY

Sea mammals are the only sea creatures that look after their young, but the rest have ingenious ways of protecting their eggs.

Why don't all sea creatures care for their young

Most sea creatures produce thousands of eggs at a time – and fertilise them in the water, where ocean currents quickly whisk them away. This makes looking after eggs and the young impossible. Some animals do care for their eggs: the octopus stays with her eggs for two months until they hatch.

How do sea mammals rear their young

Sea mammals are pretty much like us humans: the females are pregnant and then give birth. Whales and dolphins are pregnant for up to 18 months. Their 'calves' can swim right after birth. The mothers care for their young for a year, feeding them milk and protecting them from predators.

A young dolphin will stay with its mother for a year.

The female octopus stays with her eggs until they hatch.

FACT BYTES

The eggs of small sea creatures hatch as tiny larva and drift with the ocean currents. They are called plankton.

Whale and dolphin calves are a mottled colour to camouflage them from predators.

How do squid protect their eggs ❓

Squid travel hundreds of miles to gather together in their hundreds of thousands to reproduce. The female releases millions of tiny eggs into the water. The eggs are coated in a poisonous jelly. This protects them from the sharks, whales and dolphins that come to feast on the exhausted parents!

Squid

What is the largest fish egg ❓

The whale shark has the largest egg in the world – it is 36 cm (14 in.) long. A shark egg is fertilised inside the womb but then hatches and grows there too. The shark 'pup' survives by eating other eggs and pups. It swims away from the mother immediately after birth.

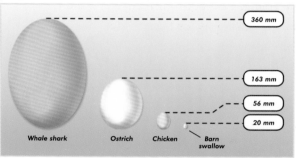

360 mm
163 mm
56 mm
20 mm

Whale shark   Ostrich   Chicken   Barn swallow

A whale shark's egg as compared to those of other creatures

FACT BYTES

Basking sharks are pregnant for 3.5 years and have the largest shark pups – 1.6 m (5.5 ft).

It is the male seahorse that becomes pregnant.

Why is the seahorse special ❓

The seahorse is the only animal in which the father gets pregnant. The mother produces the eggs, but they are looked after in the father's body until they hatch. He is pregnant for about 50 days. The seahorse young hatch out as tiny versions of their parents — up to 1,500 of them in some species.

HANDLE WITH CARE

Venom is the ultimate weapon in the war between predators and prey. These toxins are very powerful — as any swimmer who has come into contact with them can tell you!

Why are animals venomous ❓

Venom is a great way to protect yourself from predators – and a great way to attack prey too! The box jellyfish uses an incredibly powerful venom for both reasons. Its poison kills prey immediately. This stops the victim, caught up in the jellyfish's deadly but delicate tentacles, from damaging them. Symptoms of a sting may include burning, swelling, breathing problems and sometimes even a heart attack!

A box jellyfish

How can you tell if something is venomous ❓

Unfortunately, life is tough when it comes to poison; you can't always tell. The stonefish is well camouflaged and easy to step on – but it is also extremely deadly! Colour is sometimes a warning: the small, bright-blue blue ring octopus can bite through a wetsuit and kill you in minutes.

FACT BYTES

The colourful lionfish has stunning fins and spines. On the coral reef, however, it's the ultimate bully – pushing smaller fish into corners before stinging them to death.

Only the size of a golf ball, the blue-ringed octopus is lethal to humans.

The stonefish is the most poisonous fish in the sea.

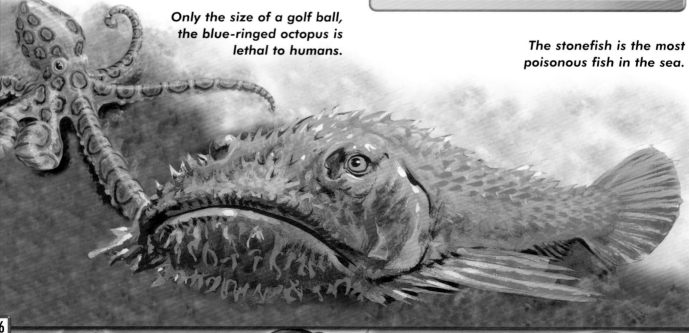

Why should you be careful picking up shells ❓

Cone snails live in beautiful coloured shells – you might like the look of one and pick it up to take home. The snail inside the shell, however, has teeth that are sharper than harpoons. These teeth can penetrate clothing and their venom can paralyse breathing and then kill.

A cone shell

How do you treat a jellyfish sting ❓

Prevention is always the best medicine. The box jellyfish's venomous tentacles react with chemicals on human skin, so it is a very good idea to cover your body when swimming in Australia. Many beaches there have vinegar dispensers – because pouring vinegar on the stung area kills the jellyfish's stinging cells.

The box jellyfish has venomous tentacles.

Which is the most venomous sea creature ❓

You have virtually no chance of surviving the venomous sting of the 'sea wasp' box jellyfish. Not only is the venom powerful enough to kill a cow in three minutes – the pain is so bad that you will probably die of shock long before you make it back to the beach.

FACT BYTES

The sting from a sea wasp jellyfish could kill 60 adults.

SCIENCE AND THE SEA

The story of Earth's past, present and future can be read in the oceans. Everything from the fate of dolphins to cures for disease may be hiding in the depths.

Why study sea creatures ?

Life evolved from the ocean, so to understand our past properly we need to look at ocean animals. Ocean life is more sensitive to change than life on land, so studying sea creatures allows us to see the changes caused by pollution – and stop them before they cause more harm.

FACT BYTES

The study of animals and plants that live in the ocean is called marine biology.

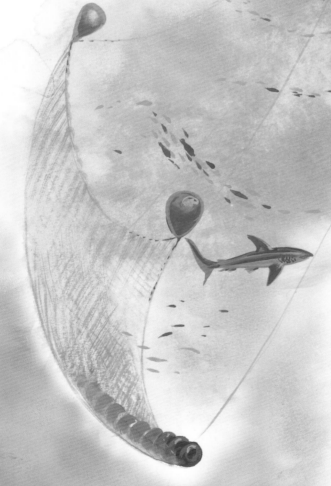

Studying ocean life can tell us much about the state of our planet.

What do they tell us about global warming ?

Study of the ocean's plankton tells scientists that extra solar radiation is killing off the organisms that sea animals feed on. This radiation is caused by global warming. In 20 years there may be no fishing and lots of hungry people – because the animals that feed on plankton will die too.

How can they help improve human health ?

Scientists often call the ocean a 'living laboratory' because sea animals can be studied quite easily. Sea animals are built more simply than land animals, so scientists can find out how living tissue works and why organs go wrong. Research on sharks has led to better blood pressure and heart drugs.

FACT BYTES

Early deep-sea machines called 'diving bells' were simple spheres of solid steel, built to withstand extreme water pressure.

How do scientists study sea creatures

Scientists trawl up marine animal specimens in trawler nets. They also use cameras on remote control vehicles to get pictures of deep-ocean creatures. Scientists can even go to the depths themselves in submarines called 'submersibles'. These machines have robotic arms and special equipment to bring live specimens to the surface.

What are the scientists working on now ?

Quite a lot is known about 50,000 marine species – but there is a lot more to find out about! Small fish called minnows are helping develop drugs that can treat children with lead poisoning. Keeping an eye on the effects of environmental change on ocean creatures is very important too.

Marine biologists study the ocean.

Remote control vehicles help us to explore the ocean.

FACT BYTES

Satellite images of the oceans tell us lots about changing weather patterns.

SCIENCE AND THE SEA

THE RESOURCEFUL OCEAN

Next time you eat fish fingers or use gas heating, remember that these good things come from the sea. The ocean is the world's greatest natural resource.

How much fish do we catch ?

Fish is highly nutritious and the major source of animal protein for humans. The fishing industry provides 30 million jobs worldwide. Each year 63 to 68 million tonnes of fish are caught – that's the weight of 1,618 *Titanic* ships. Most of this isn't for human consumption – it is used for animal feed. Overfishing is a serious issue.

An enormous amount of fish is caught each year.

Where are fish caught ?

Most fish are caught in parts of the ocean called 'upwellings'. In an upwelling, deep-ocean water meets a 'coastal shelf' (the part of a landmass that is underwater). This sends plankton-rich water to the surface. The Peruvian upwelling is the richest – it contains 66,000 times more fish than the open ocean.

The ocean around Peru contains many fish.

A trawler is used to catch several tonnes of fish.

What is modern fishing like ?

For centuries, little fishing boats would set out from coastal villages every night. They would catch small loads close to shore. Nowadays, enormous, mechanised ships called trawlers – owned by international companies – fish the ocean far from shore. They use fish-seeking radar to catch 320 tonnes of fish at one go.

FACT BYTES

The first marine parks are now open. These protect specific ocean environments from fishing and other industries. We need to do more to protect the marine environment.

How long will fish last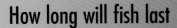

We are catching so many fish every year that we could easily drain the oceans of fish within 20 years. This is partly because of the 'drift nets' used by huge fishing trawlers. These nets trap everything that's in the water – all the way from the surface to the sea floor.

The ocean is a wonderful resource but humans must take greater care of it. Man-made pollution leads to the death of many of the ocean's creatures.

What other ocean resources are there

Fish aren't the only resource in the ocean. There are oil, gas and mineral deposits hidden under the sea floor. The ocean is also a great resource for all sorts of tourism, from beach holidays to leisure boats. Using these resources inevitably means destroying the places where sea animals live.

ENDANGERED SPECIES

When the members of an animal species die faster than they reproduce, the species can become extinct. Humans are making this happen all the time – how do we stop ourselves?

What sea animals are endangered species

Unfortunately, there are hundreds of marine animals on the endangered species list, including species of whales and sharks, five of the seven species of sea turtles, sea otters, and Australian sea lions.

Why are species endangered

Throughout time, species have become extinct, which means 'died out'. Scientists estimate that over 90% of the species that ever existed have become extinct. Recently, however, it has been humans that have been causing many of these extinctions. This is because we have been over-hunting or over-fishing, destroying natural habitats and polluting the environment.

What can we do to save animals

Some endangered species recover their numbers, others disappear forever. There is little we can do once numbers fall beyond a certain point. 'Dolphin Friendly' fishing practices have helped the spotted dolphin's population to recover.

A trapped dolphin

A spotted dolphin — populatic recovering

A manatee — 'vunerable'

A sea cow — 'vunerable'

A queen conch — extremely overfished and threatened

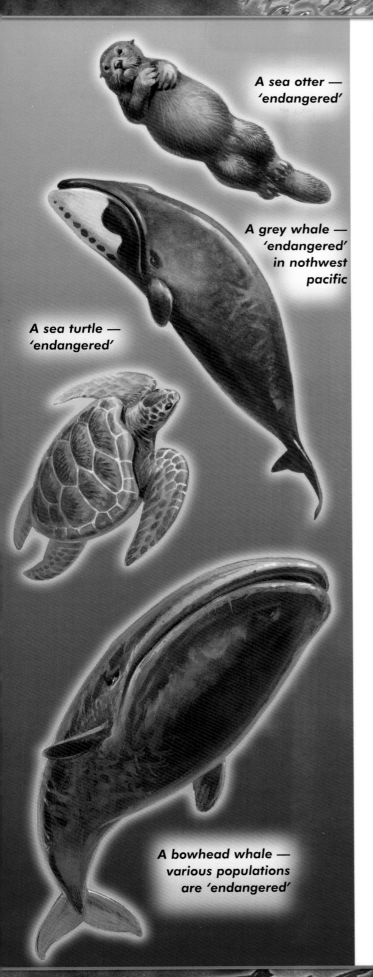

A sea otter — 'endangered'

A grey whale — 'endangered' in nothwest pacific

A sea turtle — 'endangered'

A bowhead whale — various populations are 'endangered'

Which is the cutest endangered sea animal ❓

Sea otters are sleek and furry and 1.3 m (4 ft) long. They spend most of their time in Pacific Ocean bays cracking open clams on rocks. They are fast and graceful swimmers. Unfortunately, oil spills cause their fur to lose its waterproof quality – and the otter then dies of the cold.

FACT BYTES

Grey whales were called 'devilfish' by whalers because they fought so ferociously for their lives. They have a layer of blubber up to 25 cm (10 in.) thick.

The coelacanth (below), a 380-million year old fish, was thought to have become extinct with the dinosaurs – but then turned up in the Indian Ocean!

How many whales are left ❓

Most whale hunting has now been banned and some populations are recovering, but some may never recover. There are about 15,000 right whales left – they were heavily hunted because they were easy to catch and they floated after being killed. There are about 24,000 bowheads, 12,000 blues, 80,000 humpbacks and 20,000 grey whales. Japan, Norway and Iceland continue to allow hunting.

ENDANGERED SPECIES

FISHY FACTS

You might find some of these fantastic facts hard to believe – but they are all absolutely true!

Which are the fastest fish ❓

The swordfish and marlin reach speeds of 120 km/h (75 mph), leaving the sailfish trailing behind. It reaches a top speed of 110 km/h (68 mph), folding its fins – even the biggest – into its body to move quicker. The third fastest fish is the 88-km/h (55-mph) bluefin tuna.

FACT BYTES

The shell of the chambered nautilus has a beautiful and mathematically perfect pattern on it. The pattern is called a logarithmic spiral.

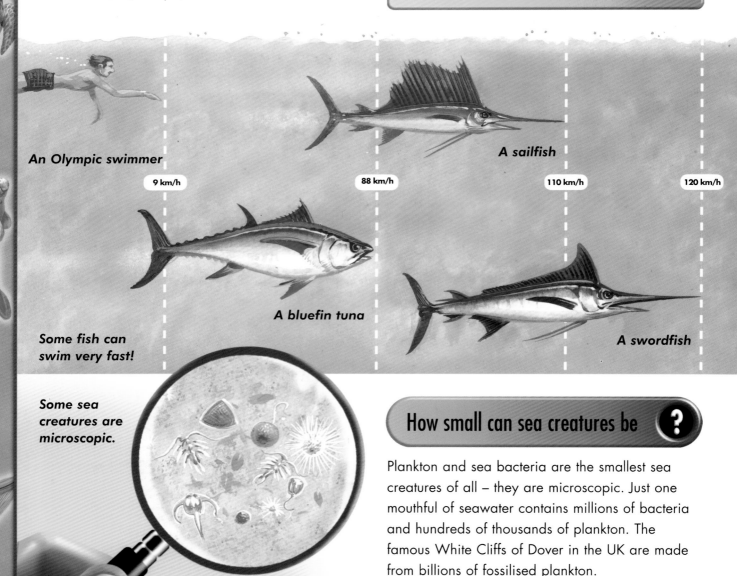

An Olympic swimmer

9 km/h

88 km/h

110 km/h

120 km/h

A sailfish

A bluefin tuna

A swordfish

Some fish can swim very fast!

Some sea creatures are microscopic.

How small can sea creatures be ❓

Plankton and sea bacteria are the smallest sea creatures of all – they are microscopic. Just one mouthful of seawater contains millions of bacteria and hundreds of thousands of plankton. The famous White Cliffs of Dover in the UK are made from billions of fossilised plankton.
The word 'plankton' comes from a Greek word meaning 'drifting'.

How weird does fish behaviour get ?

The four-winged flying fish thinks it's a bird – and flies over the waves for 400 m (1,300 ft). Starfish eat by sliding their stomachs into their prey.

A porcupine fish

The porcupine fish turns into a prickly balloon when it is attacked; dead sharks have been found with puffed-up porcupinefish still stuck in their throats.

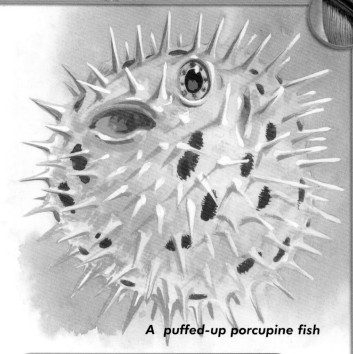

A puffed-up porcupine fish

A four-winged flying fish

Who finds the strangest uses for fish ?

The ancient Greeks applied electric rays to their bodies to numb the pain of childbirth. Indigenous Caribbeans used stingray tails on spears. Shark corneas are used in human eye surgery. The pufferfish is extremely poisonous – the liver is 1,000 times deadlier than cyanide – but considered a delicacy in Japan.

A stingray tail used on a spear

What are some amazing ocean facts ?

The ocean is an amazing place with some incredible statistics. The world's oceans produce just over 70% of Earth's oxygen. The ocean deep goes 11 km (6.86 miles) down, while the top of Mount Everest is only 8.8 km (5.49 miles) high. The longest mountain range in the known universe lies deep in the ocean. It is 64,372 km (40,000 miles) long.

The ocean is deeper, in places, than the height of Mount Everest.

GLOSSARY

Abyssopelagic
The 4,000 to 6,000 m depth zone of the ocean.

Ambergris
A pale grey, waxy substance with a strong smell produced in the intestines of sperm whales, found in lumps floating on the water or washed ashore.

Ampullae
The ampullae of Lorenzini are electroreceptive organs positioned in the head of a shark. These electrical field sensing devices are jelly-filled pores which enable a shark to detect the presence of another living creature even if all its other senses are deactivated.

Atoll
A ring-shaped coral reef surrounding a lagoon.

Coastal shelf
The part of a landmass that is under the water.

Coelacanth
The 400 million-year-old fossil fish which predates the dinosaurs; and is the closest link between fish and the first amphibian creatures which made the transition from sea to land in the Devonian period. It was first discovered in 1938.

Cookie cutter shark
This mid to deep sea dweller is named after the neat, 'cookie-shaped' wounds that it leaves on the bodies of larger fish. It grows up to 50 cm long and has a cigar-shaped body and a conical snout.

Diving bell
A large, hollow, bottomless, underwater container pumped full of air, to

which an unequipped diver returns to take in oxygen.

Dugong
A grey-brown, whale-like, plant-eating tropical sea mammal that lives for up to 50 years and grows up to 3 m in length.

Epipelagic zone
The 0 to 200 m depth zone of the ocean.

Food chain
A sequence of organisms arranged in such a way that each feeds on the organism below it in the chain, and serves as a source of food for the organism above it.

Gravitational pull
This is what causes waves and tides, because as the Moon moves around Earth it pulls water upwards on the near side of Earth and downwards on the far side; but the

downforce is weaker.

Hadalpelagic zone
The 6,000 m plus depth zone of the ocean.

Invertebrates
Any animal lacking a backbone.

Krill
A tiny, shrimp-like shellfish or crustacean, around 15 to 30 mm long, that is eaten by whales. Krill is a Norwegian word meaning whale food.

Logarithmic spiral
As in the nautilus snail where each new chamber of its shell is a fixed percentage larger than the previous one.

Mariana trench
This is located in the Pacific Ocean not far from Japan. It is the deepest part of Earth's oceans and

the deepest location of Earth itself. Its deepest point is called the Challenger Deep.

Mesopelagic zone
The 200 to 1,000 m depth zone of the ocean.

Narwhal
An Arctic whale; the male has a long, spiral tusk.

Nudibranch
Also known as sea slugs because they are like snails without shells. Many are brightly coloured, others are more subtly coloured and therefore easily camouflaged. They are some of the most beautiful creatures in the ocean and there are some 3,000 different species.

Pangaea
The name given to the hypothetical 'supercontinent' that is thought to have represented the entire landmass of Earth about 200 to 250 million years ago; before it split into separate continents.

Panthalassa
The ocean that surrounded the surface of Earth hundreds of millions of years ago before it divided into five oceans.

Photosynthesis
A process whereby green plants manufacture carbohydrates from carbon dioxide and water using the light energy from sunlight trapped by the pigment chlorophyll.

Plankton
Microscopic animals and plants that float or drift with the current in the surface waters of seas and lakes. Plankton are an important food source for invertebrates, fish and whales and form the basis of all marine food chains.

Pod
This is the name given to the closely-knit family groups of killer (orca) whales which consist of up to 30 members. They swim together, usually no more than 1 km apart.

Primeval
Something that belongs to Earth's beginnings; in other words, from the earliest age or ages.

ROVs
Remotely operated vehicles.

Submersible
A vessel that is able to operate successfully under water.

Symbiosis
The close association between two organisms of different species, usually to the benefit of both partners. Mostly this relationship is essential for their mutual survival.

Trilobite
An extinct marine arthropod having a flat, oval body divided lengthwise into three sections. Also, the fossilised remains of this animal.

Upwellings
Caused by a process in which cold, often nutrient-rich water from the ocean depths rises to the surface.

GLOSSARY

INDEX